# The North End of the Possible

ANDREW PHILIP was born in Aberdeen in 1975
and grew up near Falkirk. His first full collection
of poetry, *The Ambulance Box* (Salt, 2009), was
shortlisted for the Aldeburgh First Collection Prize,
the Seamus Heaney Centre Prize for Poetry and
in the Scottish Book Awards. His work has been
published in the UK, US and Ireland, translated
into Italian and included in anthologies such as *The
Forward Book of Poetry 2010*, *The Best British Poetry
2011* and *Adventures in Form*. He is poetry editor at
Freight Books, a Scots language editor at *Irish Pages*
and a popular online tutor for the Poetry School.

ALSO BY ANDREW PHILIP

POETRY CHAPBOOKS
*Tonguefire* (HappenStance, 2005)
*Andrew Philip: A Sampler* (HappenStance, 2008)

POETRY COLLECTIONS
*The Ambulance Box* (Salt, 2009)

# The North End
# of the Possible

*by*

ANDREW PHILIP

*for Shirley,*

*Best wishes,*

27/05/13

SALT

CROMER

PUBLISHED BY SALT PUBLISHING
12 Norwich Road, Cromer, Norfolk NR27 0AX

© Andrew Philip, 2013

The right of Andrew Philip to be identified as the
author of this work has been asserted by him in accordance
with Section 77 of the Copyright, Designs and Patents Act 1988.

Salt Publishing 2013

Printed in Great Britain by the MPG Books Group, Bodmin and King's Lynn

Typeset in Paperback 9 / 13

ISBN 978 1 907773 41 9 hardback

1 3 5 7 9 8 6 4 2

*for Judith*

# Contents

# Acknowledgements

Acknowledgements are due to the editors of the following magazines and anthologies where some of these poems, or versions of them, first appeared: *5PX2: Five Italian Poets and Five Scottish Poets* (Edizioni Torino Poesia and Luath Press), *A New Orkney Anthology* (The George Mackay Brown Writing Fellowship), *By Grand Central Station We Sat Down and Wept* (Red Squirrel Press), *Gutter, Horizon Review, Irish Pages, Magma, Silk Road Review,* and *Split Screen: Poems Inspired by Film and Television* (Red Squirrel Press).

Many thanks to Rob A Mackenzie, Jane McKie, Mark Burnhope, Tony Williams and Ira Lightman for their comments and suggestions.

Many thanks to Alastair Cook and Douglas Robertson for their work on the filmpoem of poems from this book. See: http://vimeo.com/alastaircook/macadam

I am grateful to Creative Scotland for the receipt of a writer's bursary, without which this book would not have been completed.

Profound thanks also go to Kristin Linklater for her transformational voice workshop at Cove Park.

# The North End
# of the Possible

# MacAdam's First Act of Environmental Courage

Shortcutting down a gloomed-out close,
MacAdam finds the past 12 months'
unused moons wheelie-binned outside
the back door of a dealership:

moons for howling or winching by,
moons for fishing out of gutter pools
on a Friday night, moons that sing
a song about I love you, moons

made of Wensleydale, papier mâché,
silver paint, moons of understated beauty
and moons with a faulty connection
to the motherboard. Aware of the lack

of local facilities for lunar recyclate,
MacAdam opens his pockets
to jostle the lot in amidst the detritus
he's gathered – the unheard knocking

of a pantomime horse, a portrait
of the author as an official demand
for chocolate and the unknown
comedian's failed last laugh –

thinking: *If all that reflected light
was landfilled, would everyone see
how much was going to waste?*

# A Child's Garden of Physics (1)

Trauchled by the paraphernalia
of a life spent tinkering
– the long stands, the mundae hammers –
MacAdam settles

to cobbling light apart
into constituent darknesses:
pit mirk, pick mirk, part mirk, heart mirk.
Even so, there's hardly

enough mirk in this world
to account for the breadth of black
he thinks must lie
at the core of everything.

And here it is, nestling
in the pleasant land of Counterfact,
spreading as the sun droops:
the fundamental particle of night.

It shades in/out of being
the way MacAdam does when not
observing himself at a distance,
his anchor ego flowing

through various queerlike states
akin to the nocton's flavours:
still, thrang, change, dread,
silent and sudden. The quirks

the hour has flung at him
gather in the corner of his shed.
Now, armed with the tools
to measure the mirk aright,

he can take to the streets
to ascertain precisely what
the afterlight is made of – this
could be his service to us all.

# MacAdam Essays the Truth of Each Dichotomy

Our man unsilos a sample of the night,
cupping it as a child would do
a creature scooped from a cage or pond.

If he blows on it, soft or hard,
will it redden like a coal
or turn a deeper, more dazzling dark?

If he lets it loose into the day, will it
rise to the rooftops and spread
– a mirk eagle raxing its wingspan –

or slink towards the sewer and form
a gooey, glaurie dub?
If he birls it round his head at speed,

will it wheech to the furthest reach
or splodge on the closest wall?
If he keeps it cooried in his palms,

will it live another hour? So many
choices, MacAdam,
and none without a smack of risk.

# *A Child's Garden of Physics (2)*

Against his every expectation
and counter to his careful plans,
MacAdam's next experiment succeeds
in creating a cluster of antinoctons.

*Correction: you did not create us,*
they insist. *We were here before*
*you ignited our potential.*

*You'd find us if only you knew*
*where to look. For instance,*
*each time you consume*

*a slab of Green & Blacks,*
*you bite us into being. But we*
*are squeezed by the march*

*of the nocton and we know not why.*
*Will you delve for us more deeply*
*in the heart of anti-unreality?*

*We can promise you no glory bar*
*your own private pride. We can promise*
*plenty ridicule and pain.*

## MacAdam Essays the
## Epistemics of a Dream

It used to chase me through the dark each night,
though the dark was a crowded beach dizzy with sun
and I was never alone but running with my father
and it was two men dressed in dark suits
who were agents of HM secret services
though how this was known to me I couldn't tell
and why we were the quarry I could never say
nor whether we had any chance
or where my mother and siblings had been left
on the jam-packed beach and whether they
were safe or held by others dressed in dark suits
and why no one on the baking sands
ever seemed perturbed to see two suited men
chase a small boy and his father
among picnic bags and sandcastles,
windbreaks, beach towels and changing room queues
to what end or ending none could ever state.

# A Child's Garden of Physics (3)

Something of the night leaches
from MacAdam's shed and turns
the herb garden agin itself:

bittermint and rankmary
lavendire and purple rage
swippertly choke the beds:

foulpeas thrive, thunderflowers
turn their faces from the sun
while each and every thorn

strauchles to find its rose.
Now MacAdam, who has never
been sent a rose – and what

would he do with such a bloom
but sit and watch the petals
drop? – stands helpless

at the centre of this wave
as his lawn brittles and blackens,
as the blight stalks further

down the street and out
towards a town on the brink
of waking.

# MacAdam Takes to the Road

Thirteen miles to empty and no petrol in sight,
but MacAdam must keep driving, past
new builds halted by recession,
office walls opened to the wind,
wisps of insulation tumbleweeding the highway,
mothballed factories skirting the town,
scrapyard hoards of rusting bodywork,
old freight lines taken out of service,
and hogweed hounding the wounded horizon
even though he knows he soon will shiver
to a stop and strand himself
in this edgeland chill, dreaming of everything
made fresh, made whole, fulfilled.

# MacAdam Takes to the Sea

Unhooked from its tenter, the sea drifts off
to arrive at a new understanding
with the earth
              while MacAdam, wearied
and clean out of Red Bull,
                   walks to the edge
of the land he's always called home.

Pure force of habit, that locution:
                      he has come
to feel more at home on the move these days –
on the move and in the dark.

                         Aye, but there's dark
and dark the dawn has marvelled at.
It's hidden from him yet, but MacAdam
must drive through such a gloom
to witness how
              lightly the morning rises from its knees.
For now,
         we leave him wading
waist deep into the loosened waves.

# *Renewables*

Sleek white singers of the skyline,
                    hither and yon
          you appear
crowded in chorus and lauding

the wind for its pressure and speed.
                    So few hear
          your voices
even filtered through the grid:

how can we tell if your rank and file
                    could ever prevail
          against the breakers
massed at our littoral fears?

# *Personal Space*

*for Robert Peake*

We bigg wirsels a hame in-
atween wirds whaur we
feel maist hail

the wey a bodie micht
construct hissel a beild
i' the maist nairra space

and place his pillae in yae
corner    his wardrobe i' the ither;
micht set his muckle gless

on an auld Persian rug
aside a lang reid
matchstick and then paint

the whitest cloods slawly
driftin ower ilka inch
o his blue obliterate waws

[11]

# Look North (and North Again)

Since the result of
the referendum on
the fate of Berwick-upon-Tweed,
there have been increasing reports that adults

in Northern England
are spontaneously
becoming Scottish. Doctors state
that the condition does not seem infectious

but they are baffled
by its rapid spread south
and the fact that most patients show
no previous connection to, or even

predilection for,
Bonnie Scotland the Brave –
duillich, chan eil fhios agam de
thachair an sin. The Scottish Government is

said to be working
round the clock in order
to isolate the cause so that
the effect can be marketed to tourists.

Claims that the disease
originated in
a particularly braw herd
o Aberdeen Angus immediately sent

sales skyrocketing
in North America,
but Westminster has responded
by skelpin an export ban on aw Scots fuid.

Although Number 10
is said to be sair fashed
aboot the menu for the Queen's
official banquet in Holyrood the morn,

the palace brushed aff
contamination fears
and revealed plans tae welcome guests
wi the traditional Auld Reekie hailson,
*Ye'll have had yer tea.*

# MacAdam's Inventory
# o a Tourist Trap

Fully pleyable Celtic hairps.
Robert the Bruce's dunnerin hairt.

Flatpack kists o Stirling Brig
wi clear assembly, written in Pict-

ograms. The *Scotochronicon* in Ur-Glaswegian.
Stanes o Destiny, repatriation

in wi the price. Plastic kilts.
Haggis-flavoured chocolate keich.

The Honours o Scotlan, haun picked
for waddings, birthdays and Burns nichts.

(Nou in stock:
de luxe edition wi Walter Scott.)

Colloquial Gaelic in Three Myths.
Genuine sporran, complete wi moths.

John Knox voodoo dolls made wi yer breiks.
A brief, dreich guide tae life in Leith.

Wi purchases ower the price o a dram,
a complementary clearance fae wir factor's man.

# Tae a Lousy Piper

*on seein him crawl up the Royal Mile*

Mishanter faw yer crabbit face,
great golach o the pipin race.
Afore St Giles ye tak yer place
    wi ither gowks
there for tae blaw an pech an skraich
    for furrin fowk.

When you stairt up, the lift shuid fill
wi groans fae them that has tae thole
yer total want o tunin skill,
    yer connacht reeds,
the mankit time ye stamp out ill
    wi muckle feet.

But it's photaes taen, siller skailt
intil yer gantin case that waits
for unsuspectin tourist bait
    that cannae tell
gin whit ye play is worth its weight
    or straucht fae hell.

I'v never heard sic constipation,
sic wersh, wanchancy emanation
fae this braw emblem o ma nation
    as you purvey.
Nou, this micht come as a revelation
    but – ye cannae play.

[15]

The ugsome din ye pass for pipin
wid fleg an fash the fiercest Viking.
Nae maitter that he's yaised tae skitin
    gleg throu battle,
the pair auld craitur wid gang gyte an
    sned his thrapple!

O wid some pooer the giftie gie ye
tae hear yersel as ithers hear ye!
I threap it wid dae nocht tae free ye
    fae yer glaikit notions.
Truth is, I wid prefer tae see ye
    faur ower the ocean.

Sae listen here: enough's enough.
I dinnae hae tae thole sic guff.
An nou thir lines has caaed yer bluff,
    juist haud yer wheesht.
Pack up yer pipes, syne bummle aff
    an gie us peace!

# Nocturne to 60 in 10 Seconds

*for Judith*

Tossing and turning in a strange bed, I
can't help but think of you so fast asleep
nothing would rouse you from the deep
recesses of your dreams except a cry
of hunger or pain from the child who lies
beside you in a Moses basket, sweet
awake but sweeter still asleep. Our street's
as hushed and empty as the midnight skies

till some boy racer revving round its circuit
shatters all thought of rest for the open eyed.
Although it's just by chance you haven't heard it
– that sole competitor outpacing pace
without respect for our few hours of peace –
I know I'd sleep more soundly by your side.

# 10 × 10

*for Judith*

## 1. ORIGAMI

You are a folded deer quick-stepping
the bog-cotton muir of a how-to book.
Hind for the white hart whose leathery heart you have
smoothed to bleaching linen or a page
freshly rolled in the mill, I adore you

for every crease unironed in your nature.
Not for me the copper-bottomed überbeauties,
those bronzed denizens of the glossies
who are glazed like fine porcelain and just as vacant
as washed tins dropped in the recycling.

## 2. SUMMERTIME . . .

Backlit by a Balkan sunset, in your denim skirt
and well-worn sandals you sit by the water's edge:
it's a favourite snap of mine. The gloaming heckles
dark from the evening, turning the trees across the bay
to pig-iron sculptures of themselves. In that light,

your hair becomes a metonym for fire, as if
burnishing the air around to a deep bronze sheen;
your smile becomes a kiln for happiness. As if
we could can that for the years ahead! Still, while we're able,
let's linger in the moment's printed afterglow.

### 3. SHAGREEN

Imagine us old: wrunkled cowhide faces,
me in linen trousers at some summer festival,
one of us walking with a stick, both chatting
with the bittersweet, gentle irony of the aged,
all trace of copper faded from your hair.

Our younger heads, cast in bronze by a friend,
may occupy a prominent spot beside your Dutch vase,
prevailing over the tinpot fears of aging
as we recall fondly the days of cheap paper,
inexpensive cotton and less heat.

## 4. THE RAVELLING

A certain group of flaxen-haired wee boys
has breached the doors of pre-school nursery.
We spy them through the railings and experience
a kick like power surging down the wires —.
Grief is no monolith. It's more like molten bronze

or a potsherd dug up in unexpected tilth.
It speeds like a tinfish out of sonar range.
It's a crack that can't be papered over
for long, a snapped thread left to hang,
a belt to scourge our each essay at happiness.

## 5. Dovetail Joints

I could never have lifted you over the threshold.
And let's not count the ways I've dropped the iron,
or mention the nail you hammered through a hot water pipe,
the sun screen I slaistered on well past its use-by. Let's not
enumerate the plates and bowls that clattered from our grasp

this past 10 year. That's all in the can. Instead,
I'm leafing through the future's wide extensions,
its beds replanted with pear trees and cotoneaster.
A suede-upholstered future, our coming years together
unfolding like a brand new pack of king-sized sheets.

## 6. Ferrous Sulphate

Dark chocolate, Guinness and steamed asparagus.
Your thickened hair basting in the summer sun,
your skin not burnished, browned or slightly burnt.
Casseroles and other one-pot dishes sitting by the door.
Tinned apricots crowding the kitchen cupboards

as if on free prescription. Red books and birth certificates.
Fitted cot sheets, muslin squares and body suits.
My footwear worn from pounding the surrounding streets.
The linens on our whirligig and no space left for drying.
How mighty oaks we hope from little acorns now are growing.

## 7. Small Change

Every red penny we save these days
is technically bronze, so nothing – not even
the humble piggy bank, or the chugger's
rattly plastic collecting tin – is quite
what it looks on paper. Nor are we

who we were when we first shared the sheets,
my kilt and sporran tossed with your dress,
the hotel linens wrapping us tight. But I
don't pine to buy those times back, not even though
what we've shared since then would temper steel.

## 8. Coming Third

Never was it gold or silver in the medal stakes.
Never bone china, always the bargain-basement crockery.
Never the full spectrum, always the tinnier speakers.
Always paper-thin ham instead of the juicier cuts;
static-filled synthetics rather than Egyptian cotton.

But now we're talking genuine Italian leather,
an Irish linen garment cut to fit just so,
African ebony inlaid with mother of pearl,
pure Ossetian free of loans and calques,
a sunstruck copper roof devoid of verdigris.

## 9. A Cut-Price Set of Crockery

Barely six months' use when the glaze cracked.
It felt as smooth as a fresh roll of kitchen foil,
an unsigned marriage certificate or
the new sheets on our first, rented bed but looked
more like withered shoes beneath museum glass.

We traced the daily strains with our dishtowels
and at the table over breakfast or dinner.
Iron sharpens iron it is written. We felt more like
a copper cup already turning green. But no:
we were a new-minted penny ready to shine.

## 10. Not Being the Woodsman of Oz

I once played the cowardly lion; a coward
not only in the script, whispered some who'd not
cottoned on – seeing how feart I was
of a playground leathering; of muddying my
clothes on the pitch; of the opposite sex – that courage

to weep could compensate. Bit of a cross to bear.
You had your crosses too, hard as nails and heavier.
They may mean you feel no Venus, but to me
you're a bronze shield cast by Vulcan or a new
earthenware goblet brimming with wine.

# *Oh, Jubilant Jute Lid!*

*An abnominal for Judith Julia Belton*

Bonnie hen, be a blue balloon
ajaunt abuin an undulate tent.

Be a jet bead, at haun no
in dool alane but attendant

in *joie*. Be the Nile Delta.
Be a beaut o a hind

nibblin on a jade hill. Ah! –
be unbuttoned. Be neat

ethanol – a libation. Be oil on
hubbub and hullabaloo. Thole nae jibe,

nae bald lie, nae indolent hate.
Bonnie jo, be Dettol and Bandaid.

Hunt total healin. Be a banjo, an oboe,
a tuba; be a ballet, a ballad tune.

Binna jejune. Be bold, held, boltholed,
haloed and hained. Binna dual,

but ane. Thole nae jail, nae hell.
Be unbiddable. Be an inundation!

In the duel anent the Lion o Judah,
be leonine. Bonnie hinnie, be attuned.

# The Melody at Night, With You

*ECM 1675*

Snow bound and determined to break
out of the silence enforced by chronic fatigue,
Jarrett is at his piano again – the first time
in let's not contemplate how long for a man
as given to his art as this – stripping
the music back to all that ever mattered,
taking it to heart the way you'd want
her to take what you know most sparing:
your softest, most unguarded speech and touch –
no smoke, no mirrors, no sleight of hand,
no firecracker runs or full-voltage solo virtuosics:
just the tune; the tune and Christmas coming.
A moment to warm the fingers. Press *RECORD*.

# MacAdam Essays the Delights
of Small-Town Life

Among splashdown crossroads
and tramline fragments,
meaningless acts are taking place.

Drunk sermons on the brink of violence,
great lines of orderliness and fast-track toasters
shatter in the hands.

One hesitation begins a chain:
MacAdam – wide eyed and blinkered,
never moving forward, never back –

ignores the shine of the times,
the cutting-edge impresarios of anything,
the declared state of paranoia.

Muzak reminds him of similar muzak
in favourite restaurants where
the angel Barbie – a bearer of absence –

forms herself from her Maker's voice.
(Casually. Everything she does is casual.)
At six degrees, it's the ideal conditions

for a Magnum in Falkirk. Fist raised,
a fallen saint, MacAdam flares in love.

# On Holding

'Let's switch energy provider for the love of it,' he said, holding on
to the handset as if to a grenade set to go off
at the moment of release. *Thank you for holding*, crackled out
from the earpiece for the nth time. She sighed: 'Stop pacing. Breathe in
and take a seat, for goodness' sake. Or else give up
for now.' 'I won't,' he growled, 'let another call centre grind me down!

'Like many – as you well know – the first job I held down
was in just such an openplan hellhole located on
the edge of the city bypass, no amenities' – 'Oh do shut up,'
she interjected, 'Bo-ring. I know all your peerie rants off
by bleeding heart.' Mumbai chipped in with *Your call is held in
our queuing system*. 'Aye, I ken,' he girned, 'When will ye let it oot?'

She lifted a book: 'Shields up, Mr Sulu. I'd hold out
for a toothsome touchtone menu: *Press 1 for a put-down
that will stoke your ire; 2 for more menus; 3 to be put in
touch with a human who'll serve your name wrong three ways.'*
　　'Just get on
with it!' he yelled at the phone. *'All our operators are off
with stress'* she quipped, *'/powdering their noses/shrivelled up.'*

'Repeat after me,' he sighed: 'life is one long hold-up.
You're born; you stay on hold; you die. Does that spell it out
neatly enough?' 'Perhaps not. You might have left something off
that list: "Your call may be recorded for training purposes."' 'Down
with training purposes, queuing systems, endless hours on
the blower listening to tinny Vivaldi pieces in

glorious mono!' he roared. 'You really should learn to hold in
your emotions a bit more, dear,' she scolded. 'This keeps me up
at night,' he confessed, calming: 'how much of life do we spend on
hold? Has no one calculated that? They always dole out
grants like sweeties for the daftest projects.' 'I would put it down
to caffeine intake.' *Your call is important to us.* 'Fuck off!'

they snorted in unison. 'I reckon you should just hold off
until tomorrow,' she smiled. 'Come to bed. You don't look good
    wrapped in
that many scowls. You've been pacing down and up, up and down
so long that carpet must be through to the boards. You'll be up
way past midnight if you keep at it, and don't forget you're out
to catch the early train.' He groaned. *All our operators are on*

*other calls. Thank you for holding. Don't put down the phone, switch off*
*your mobile or turn your back on us. Your call is held in our*
*queuing system, which won't give up until it's burned you out.*

# *Grian is Gorm*

*i.m. Derick Thomson/Ruaraidh MacThòmais*

whoever thinks,
this infinite lunch hour –
    its blazing sky
        sugared with cirrus –

of where
the great Gaelic poet is gone,
    perhaps there will be
        *eagal orra*, as with

        the *Lochlannaich*
*a' tighinn air tìr* in his poem
    of another ground,
        as the thought rises

of travelling,
*cop air bainne blàth na mara,*
    *sian nan tonn* in the ears,
        and *a' ghrian a' deàrrsadh*

    travelling
from the *sùlaire a' tuiteam á fànas,*
    the *àile liathgorm an eòrna,*
        and the *gainmheach geal,*

    travelling
into a darkness we cannot fathom
    where, at last, we may find dazzlement
    and the withering of our *cianalas*

# Silver Nitrate

*for Carl Radford*

He sluiced the darkness off. One moment
    *the process reveals*
with its inky twin, and there emerged
    *a level of detail*
on glass a stern and ghosted version
    *in a three dimensionality*
of my head and neck awaiting
    *difficult to convey unless*
sun and fixative
    *holding a plate*
to pull each pore and freckle, each pin
of beard hair through to uncommon life.

It is my face and not my face, stilled
    *those that have sat*
mirror image I witness daily
    *often express a connection*
that hides my missing in its features,
    *that other forms of capture*
in the cast of dust and ashes round
    *do not hold*
the eyes, in its lips
    *this is how they see themselves*
shut off from breath, from speech, from loosing
another's mouth with a bruising kiss.

# Bereavement fir Dummies

Bonnie, unkent boy; brucken bairn:
deid pixel at the centre o ma screen;
dichtit comment crucial tae the threid:
ye'r loast faur ben this haurd drive o a hairt –

a scartit file that bides there, fractured, dern;
that cannae be recovert, even seen.
Defrag the disk, an naethin's in the steid
I thocht wid pruive tae be yon data's airt.

But sae whit? Gin the file is delete,
the bits that biggit hit's spreid throu the kist –
an antivirus, awmaist: undaein skaith,
rebootin ilka tear it gart me greet
when we funt oot whit wey it wis ye crashed
athoot yer lungs haein ony chance o braith.

# Autumn Leaves

*At the Blue Note Vol III (ECM 1577)*

the phrase unfolds under Jarrett's fingers
a Swiss army knife of the heart fanning out
each miniature blade and tool
perfectly shaped and whetted to purpose
however obscure it might be
even to those whose survival skills
are fitted to this camsheugh world
or those with ears for the subtleties
of harmony, rhythm, the moment's felicity
and the way one dives in and out of the other
like swifts in flight that follow each avenue
choice and instinct make available
in much the same way as we live
this particular grief

                which requires

somebody else to repeat that phrase
unfolding under Jarrett's fingers
over and over

            out into the gloom
where the audience sits unseen

# Gåta

Kurt a Scotch in his claustral flat sips.
The bare case facts a mind order
in him improvise.

Elsewhere seems to be all happening:
in Nyberg's brain *overtimed*, in Linda's
love life *overturned*

at the locus *lacklustre* of the latest crime.
Deceived, dear viewer, do not be:
Waken Wallander will

to critical skelf evidence long
overlooked or scurried from his team
in nick of time.

Later, no/sooner, no. Is this what we demand
of a detective *braw* on a Saturday night:
That he be dour

as winter in Ystad; that a monkish
silence he maintain in the bulk
of scenes; that

the whole world rotten he bang
to rights by the closing credits; that he us
in turn turn in?

# The Black Itch

The classic midrash quoted by Ramban states
that Abram, as a youth, was cast into the furnace
at his father's hand. As the campaign slogan has it,

don't give fire a home. *There's always eros in errors*, such as
*lamented savings in public sector pensions*. Or is that
just a Jesuitical dance on an intellectual pinhead?

What's the ideal brand name for an e-cigarette?
We could ask the haggard workmen by the internal door,
cloaked in their own stale tobacco atmosphere,

which can be breathed in by your individual.
They're not pretending to be something they are not
– workers out there really should tell the truth –

as Bill Cudd – sorry, Bill Kidd – said earlier.
*Do you sure?* I do not sure. When we turned around,
the fireball was just forming. There it was, like a giant

sunset up in the air. Here it is again, with accents
and a magnificent beat. Philosophers have long since
stopped trying to tell us the world is fire, so may we

recommend you learn to ask better questions?
May we recommend: Fish and chips. Hot soup
to sit in or take away. *We have the fire and the wood*

*for the sacrifice, but where is the lamb?*
Sorry, kid. Zero power is definitely a selection,
but I have to compromise. God will provide alarm.

He said he did it for the good of his country.
(Where do they get those professors of law these days?)
No further conversation between them is recorded.

# *MacAdam and the 24-hour News Culture*

The powerless of another state presume themselves
on to the streets, as MacAdam watches
those he'd learnt to misbelieve
acquire the levers of powerlessness at home.

He debates the small and media mindedness
of their society, his front room given over
to the permanent infotainment revolution
he decries with regularity in posts

the length and breadth of nowhere.
Somewhere all too real, the people are dying for
the right to remain loud, the right
to circle the square of their choice.

MacAdam raises his glass to freedom
and goves at his convictions through the empty bottle.
What will he say when the time comes?
It is not far, the desert. It is not far.

# *Hum Int*

The great men looked at each other.

On the table in front of them lay a note
setting out credible intelligence

that, somewhere in the dark –
in the minds of the angry, the awkward,
the unemployed –

                a poem was growing.

They shifted in their chairs.

                        The poem
was not amenable to measurement
against capital or revenue budgets.

Their Italian suits began to chafe
at the crotch.

                    The poem was known only
to say: *Trespassers will be welcome*.

Their chilled wine could not take away the taste.

# *Extract from the Annals: The Farewell Tour*

And, having built Jerusalem,
he set about dismantling {*these*

*lines have been defaced and are
no longer decipherable*} dozed on

through sleight of headline,
gradual twists of speech or evidence

and {*an improvised erasive device
has rendered this clause illegible*}

eventually glad-handing it across
the small screens of the globe —

olive branch and hymn book
in one fist, while {*we regret that*

*damage is necessary*} to the other,
the requisition orders for an empire.

# The White Dot

A blink of frenzy on the living room screen as rescuers
haul the last known survivor from reinforced dust

where her house once stood: at over 100 years old
she's already witness and survivor of more

than most would care to imagine, especially the young
reporter who, elsewhere in the stricken province, presses

a cordless phone into the hands of a trapped man so she
can beam his last conversation round the franchised globe

as his voice falters and gives out. On another channel
someone's claiming to speak to the dead between adverts

but who can really tell if anybody's there to listen
and whether after is so much better than before?

Meantime, in a stricken province elsewhere, the masses
have gathered to stake their claim on the hearse of a poet

and his refusal to be shackled by facts on the ground
or factions growing fat on such bloody sterilities

while viewers in the starstruck provinces ask
the big questions of the day. But each of us

switches off eventually, like an old cathode ray set,
its picture dwindling to that tiny white dot

before the blackness. *Now*, MacAdam thinks,
*it's all so slick: sleek flat LCD sets in front rooms,*

*great big plasma screens dotted about the city –*
*nothing to fixate on as the box powers down.*

# *Breathing is the Place to Start*

Let everything
        have breath.

        Let there be
     no limit but
the next lungful.

Let silence
        be the only thing
        to fall silent,

        even the grave
     become glad
with laughter

as God the mother
        lifts to her face
        chaos

        for that first
     fond kiss.

# *Consanguineous*

Easy doesn't : we're all in
this tomorrow : shoulder
to shoulder and eye for
a ruddy great bruise

the sandwich board's end
is nigh on the agenda : replacement :
tweeting : vengeance is mined
( bottom-sneaking pelagic tinfish

pulse their ways round earth )
but now : I say  I say  I say : what
do you get when you turn
the other : cheek of it : when

judgement arrives : an order
placed for restoration furniture
the true colour of dried blood
( cold, deep waters show no mercy )

# MacAdam Takes to the Sky

### 1. GEALBHONN

Through thunder, smirr
and the threat of sun, MacAdam
sits six days and nights in his garden
holding a tiny knitted bird

to which he trusts each hope
of finding a way to unburden
his chip-poke soul, queasy with
the residue of life on the town.

## 2. FAOILEANN

MacAdam tells the bird:
*A man cannot live*
*from the deep fat fryer alone,*
but with every word, gulls

cackle closer. He lifts his *gealbhonn*
to the gloaming and feels
a sudden windflichter
at his whummled face.

### 3. CLAMHAN

MacAdam minds his childhood
dream of spread arms swooping
down the stairs and how it was
nothing like this narcotic

rush of air beneath the oxters,
this taking hold of the lift
with bare hands and shaking
till all the clouds erupt.

## 4. UISEAG

Somehow, MacAdam feels
at home in this unbound element,
unfankling gravity
at the north end of the possible,

rehearsing the love of thermals
up among the cirrus,
twittering his joy with the best
of the open-throated *eòin*.

## 5. SPIDEAG

Nightingales flock from their perches
and laverocks soar to sample
MacAdam's supple if camsteerie song,
while wild geese chase him

heeliegoleerie through the skies,
willing his lead to thunder on
but knowing well the time
will come for its demise.

## 6. SÙLAIRE

Six days and nights in the air,
and MacAdam wearies
for a taste of salt and sauce,
the promise of crunch

held out by the perfect batter.
The gannets haul gifts
– herring and mackerel –
fresh from the open sea.

## 7. FAOILEAG

Nothing those bombdivers bring
satisfies MacAdam's aching wame.
Seamaws skraich directions
to the finest scavenging points

and he airts his body back
at the unbekent ground.    This was
the seventh day: MacAdam arrested
on suspicion of something unspoken.

# Cheer Friend of Both

*An abnominal for Dietrich Bonhoeffer*

Thorn in the *Reich*, be the torch
for the terrified bride

of the torn *Herrn*. Interned,
confined, be free in the other

hidden *Reich*, the one eterne.
If the dirt of the *Hof* be

bitter herb, *bete doch*
*'For thine be —.'*

*Ich hoffe* not trite: no richer effort
to render the terror inert. Brief

the trot to *Tod*. Therefore, brother,
be fortified, cheered, enriched.

Deride the thin, horrid, inferior credo
ordered. Be interior hobo, freed

to intent. Tend the bidden boon.
If it be no *Hilfe*, do not ochone;

ochone for the *Eiche*, the *Erde*,
the bent *Hirte*. No introit intoned, be

the *Brot* bitten: be rid of, interred.
Thorn in the *Reich*, be reborn.

[54]

# MacAdam Incarcerate

Nothing like the death of sleep
to finish a man, and MacAdam
is worn to his weft with worry,
pacing round this untried cell.

No one can pin a misdeed on him
but still he must sweat the hours,
each a hissing fuse
exploding into its neighbour.

Through the window, he can make out
stuckies ringtoning the dawn
and the odd corbie phoning a friend
to pass on news of the new-slain night.

MacAdam lives in terrorhope
of a key jingling in the door;
his gaolers    dispensing grace
without mercy, mercy without grace;

the oncome of a fractured dream
to bear him over midnight's thrashel.

# MacAdam's Interrogation

*You have the right to remain silent.*
We can all talk when we have our heads on.

*Where have you come from?*
A complicated nuisance of light.

*What brought you here?*
Listening to the story in my eyes.

*What do you know of the place?*
Electric trains stop here.

*Where were you headed?*
My last wanting choice: the last lost green space.

*What do you know of the place?*
It is still wandering and still not the goal.
There are circles like that.

INTERVIEW #2

*You have the right to remain silent.*
The world begins with each and every breath.

*What do you understand of your situation?*
A bluebottle dancing round a naked bulb.

*Do you understand the gravity of your situation?*
The list is wrong.
No more can be required of us than we are given.

*What have you been given?*
The laundry list of the long-distance runner.

*Have you spoken to the widow?*
The past and the future are falling together.
There are circles like that.


INTERVIEW #3

*You have the right to remain silent.*
Unwrite this: silent except for the resonance.

# The Defence Drafts a Missive for MacAdam's Local Rag

Dear friends and neighbours of MacAdam,
  it has been a long time,
     has it? In that case,
imagine how you'd feel in his shoes.

  No – that's not what I meant:
    imagine all your
hoagie nebs jagging through the curtains,
  your gathered, tichtened een
    paparazzi-ing

each movement each moment of each day.
  Those of you with visions
    of red-top offers –
step away from your phantasies now!

  Will any of you see
    or raise the low-down
dollar I'm prepared to wager on
  just how deep a torture
    this case has become?

I thought as much. *Oh, but we've never*
  *had any trouble here*
    *before.* So you say.
*It's always the quiet ones.* So you

sing in your carnival
            of clishmaclavers.
Whisper this to yourselves in your beds:
    if you've any trouble
            now, who bears the blame?

# MacAdam's Homegoing

The house is an unquiet shell.


Smart money envisages a swift flit,
    possibly by moonlight.

Smart money severely underestimates
    the occupant.

Large amounts have been tendered
    for his reconstructed story.

Large numbers of voicemail messages
    are now delete.


The garden has, naturally, rebelled again.


MacAdam lacks: tea, coffee, bread
    and a sense of grievance.

Smart money assumes a prime-time
    special on the case.

Smart money may well have mis-
    understood its facts.

After a frustrated hunt for the remote,
he kills the commentary
running in his brain.

The house settles into unquiet dark.

# MacAdam Essays the Meaning of Loss

Angels chatter on aerials, masts and phone wires
around a forecourt studded with covenantal drops.
A reluctant hero, aged 18, jumps off the bus
to wild acclaim from above and is ignored

by everyone shadowing the streets this fine
early spring forenuin. MacAdam – guestimate:
21 again and counting back the way –
would be equally indifferent but that he'd know

what we are avoiding in our hero's eye:
a slendercast of all he left behind to learn
the pressure needed for a happy trigger.
Now, reader, look again: the scene is gone,

the bottom of the page a smoking barrel, empty
like MacAdam's glass, pretending on the bar
where those who know the terror of a beauty
in labour wait with the angels for a sign.

# Unquiet Time

Although he knows the door is locked
and no guest is expected,
MacAdam startles on
his favoured chair occupied
by a figure made entire
of coruscating darkness.

The mirkman's right hand grasps a hip flask,
the other dangles a brace
of whisky glasses.
He rises to greet his host
without a word of explanation, just
a cut to the straight no chaser:

*Care for a dram, MacAdam?*
The voice he hefts into the room
smacks of sour fruit
and richest bitter chocolate,
but MacAdam was never one to look
a gift malt in the bottle mouth.

*Glenan Alleish, 25-year-auld,*
the intruder grins as he pours.
*A nip 'n' a hauf.*
*Slàinte – you may well need it, pal.*
A singular distillation, this:
as it passes MacAdam's lips

he tastes no trace of the caller burn
or the dense peat bog,
not even salt air,
haar and driving, unrelenting rain:
it's the tang of barely lit days
at Ceann Tuath a' Dhìth.

*Aye, MacAdam, I've waited an age*
*tae to get this near ye,*
the mirkman says.
*Each time I got anywhere close,*
*you took to yer heels and showed me*
*ample stour for all my troubles.*

*I never saw me do it,* our man protests.
The mirkman's terse repone:
*Neither you would.*
His deep stare broadens into
surround-sound silence. Casually,
MacAdam takes another sip

and suddenly he's on the run,
pounding each element
with desperate feet
and hands that keep no grip.
It seems as though he's running
backwards through all his time.

Each shadowed instant phones home
to itself as quick as he moves,
his retrograde flight
a fumble of sorrows, the fizz
of that voice popping his lugs
*There is no . . .* until – PAM! –

he's flat on his back in some sweet field,
its grass a truer green
than true, *. . . no moment . . .*
everything growing time-lapse
into the ground around and under him,
the sharp sun condensing into night.

MacAdam panics to his feet
– at least, he tries to –
*. . . moment that is not . . .*
and finds himself – PAM! – scliddering
on a dancefloor of ocean,
his partner to the counterpointing gulls

our mirkman, whose song appears
to shape the pits and crests
of wave on wave
with a lilt that cuts like a flint chib:
*There is no moment*
*that is not held.*

MacAdam looks again. The sea
is gone. A shattered glass
caltrops the carpet.
No sign of the visitor, just his words:
*There is no moment
that is not held.*

Then – PAM! – his right arm is around
MacAdam's throat.
Each breath grows into
a threat. MacAdam reaches up,
slamming his assailant hard
on the skelfs and diamonds of glass.

*There is no moment that is not held,*
the wounded mirkman smiles.
MacAdam lurches
and is on the visitor's stomach,
in a flurry of fists and knees
spilling control like a knocked jug.

But every skelp and punch he lands
bursts out into
some exotic bloom:
passionflower, bird of paradise,
lily of the valley and rose
upon rose upon rose upon rose,

the colours more vivid than vivid,
more true than true.
Outside, the moon
presents its drab assumptions
to the easing street, no inkling
of the murder that's been born.

*There is no moment. That is.   Not held.*
The mirkman weakens. MacAdam,
puggled, pushes
through stems to the ruptured face.
*It is the.  Heart of.   Belonging.*
*It is your.  Gift.   It is all –*

And that is that. MacAdam's left
on his own in the dark
beside the messenger's remains,
which rapidly vanish beneath
the massive display of flowers.
A convert to his own enigma,
he rises to freak for a vase.

# MacAdam Takes to the Fire

*nec tamen consumebatur*

Take off your shoes and socks, MacAdam.
Surrender. Here and now, kneel
at this slender, street-corner rowan
aflame in the early evening rays.
It is any tree and, just like any tree,
is unlike any other tree. Stand
apart in its wholly undark shade.

Set down your bag and phone.
Have they become too burdensome
to schlep from door to door?
Then enter. Let this angel of the Lord
dissolve your empty diary, unread notes
into singable incense – the psalms
of an unrestricted throat.

# Skate and Samphire

The sky wavers over blues
undergoing correction in the workshop.

A fingernail wind
fiddles the door lock with a feather.

Loosing breakers overnight,
MacAdam will anchor a cyclone beneath

the beams and the ceiling rose,
Bach in the background.

His better eye has seen
a pale vessel drifting, singing

when the waves crash hard
around this non-discriminatory town

(a five inch-wide labyrinth).

A fortnight of light depression
– our blackest flower –

and, like a cirque-du-freak performer,
he falls bedlong into the geography

of the tethered body,
the frothing of mugs and mouths

as everything skint and sorrowful watches
– everything golden, good, evil and a little sick.

Man submits to the year's
most unnewsworthy quake.

Man submits to climb
a cliff summit, or summat like it.

Man submits to man,
held to the board and hammered.


My roughened, subdivided figurine,
carry my cross for me.

(Ah, it stings.)

# *Notes*

A glossary with the basic intended meanings of the Scots words used in the poems can be downloaded from http://www.andrewphilip.net/

Several poems from this collection have been made into a filmpoem by Alastair Cook in collaboration with Douglas Robertson. See: http://vimeo.com/alastaircook/macadam

Alastair Cook: http://www.alastaircook.com
Douglas Robertson: http://www.douglasrobertson.co.uk/
Filmpoem: http://www.filmpoem.com

MACADAM TAKES TO THE SEA
> Written as part of a collaborative project for the Hidden Door Festival, http://hiddendoor.org/, and made into a filmpoem by Alastair Cook. See:
> http://vimeo.com/alastaircook/macadamtakestothesea.

LOOK NORTH (AND NORTH AGAIN)
> Written in Thebbics, a syllabic stanza inspired by an arrangement of slabs in the garden at Linlithgow's Burgh Halls. The Gaelic phrase means, 'Sorry, I don't know what happened there.'

10 × 10
> This sequence, written as a present for my wife, is organised by direct or oblique reference to a list of anniversary gifts for the first 10 years of marriage: paper, cotton, leather, linen, wood, iron, copper, bronze, linen, pottery and tin.

OH, JUBILANT JUTE LID! AND CHEER FRIEND OF BOTH
The abnominal is a form I have developed using only the
letters of the dedicatee's name, each of which must appear
at least once per stanza. The poem, which is 20 lines long,
should begin and end by addressing the dedicatee in some
way. The title must also be an anagram of their name.

MACADAM ESSAYS THE DELIGHTS OF SMALL-TOWN LIFE
A cento, consisting of lines and phrases from Rob A
Mackenzie's collection *The Opposite of Cabbage* (Salt,
2009).

GRIAN IS GORM
The title means 'sun and blue'. The Gaelic phrases in the
poem are from Thomson's 'Na Lochlannaich a' tighinn air
tìr an Nis/The Norseman Coming Ashore at Ness'

| | |
|---|---|
| *eagal orra* | afraid (lit., fear on them) |
| *Lochlannaich a' tighinn air tìr* | Norseman coming ashore |
| *cop air bainne blàth na mara* | foam on the warm milk of the sea |
| *sian nan tonn* | roar of the waves |
| *ghrian a' deàrrsadh* | sun shining |
| *sùlaire a' tuiteam á fànas* | solan plunging out of space |
| *àile liathgorm an eòrna* | grey-green haze of barley |
| *gainmheach geal* | white sand |
| *cianalas* | homesickness |

SILVER NITRATE

The italicised text is drawn from a defunct 'about me' page on http://www.carls-gallery.co.uk/.

GÅTA

The title is a Swedish word for 'puzzle'.

THE BLACK ITCH

This hebdomad incorporates a couple of phrases from Dean Young's *The Art of Recklessness: Poetry as Assertive Force and Contradiction* (Graywolf Press, 2010).

HUM INT

A response to Norman MacCaig's 'Old Maps and New' written for an event celebrating the centenary of his birth. The italicised phrase is from MacCaig's poem.

MACADAM TAKES TO THE SKY

The Gaelic titles of the sections translate as follows:

| | |
|---|---|
| *gealbhonn* | sparrow |
| *faoileann* | common white gull |
| *clamhan* | kite |
| *uiseag* | skylark |
| *spideag* | nightingale |
| *sùlaire* | gannet |
| *faoileag* | black-headed gull |
| | |
| *eòin* | birds |

MacAdam's Interrogation

This includes two sentences from Karl Barth's *Dogmatics in Outline* (SCM Press, 1949) and a statement made by Danish composer Hans Abrahamsen in a Radio 3 interview.

Unquiet Time

*Glenan Alleish* (Anglicised sp.)   Glen of the Shadow
*Ceann Tuath a' Dhith*              The North End of Want

Skate and Samphire

A cento, consisting of lines and phrases from Mark Burnhope's pamphlet *The Snowboy* (Salt, 2011).